ELEMENTS

Attention schools and businesses; for discounted copies on large orders please contact the publisher directly.

Kallisto Gaia Press Inc.
1801 E. 51st Street
Suite 365-246
Austin TX 78723
info@kallistogaiapress.org
(254) 654-7205

Cover Design: Preston H. Burnett
Cover Photo:

ISBN: 978-1-952224-33-1

For my family
— Savi, Shiv, Mumma, Papa —
you're my everything

Elements

Poems

Sara Garg

Fairies fall to dust.
Foundations fracture. We fight
for our fickle dreams.

Water: Shootings

Blood is in the water.
Plasma spins away from bobbing bodies
carried into an ocean of violence,
red dissolving clear in the universal solvent.

Sharks circle, then attack with
glistening grins that tear the body apart.
All that's left is a crimson smear
dispersing in the shark's wake.

Tears fall for the body
lost to the waves of rising violence,
but they fall in silence
as their trail is washed away.

Soon, remembered only by the reservoir
3.8 billion years old
that immortalizes each soul
in a hydrogen bond.

Fire: Misinformation

A match flares, catching
Pandora's box of electronic headlines
inked with 1s and 0s,
ribboned with an extravagant twist.

The edges chip off shiny news sites,
only ash and their smoke rises,
releasing toxic fumes that invade my lungs
and beg me to inhale.

My eyes sting as I watch
faceless figures pour on more gasoline.
Others walk away, denying responsibility,
forgetting the footsteps they've left behind.

The internet combusts
to exorcize its demons.
The cloud ignites, and we choke
too late to repent our horns.

Earth: Division

We pierce her with flags:
team blue and team red.
We go to war with spears of words
that leave her only with our poisoned corpses.

We auction off pieces of her body—
Empty promises, empty lakes,
full coffers, full coffins—
as our drills burst her veins.

We scoff at her tears.
We offer her cloaks of smoke
and laugh when she chokes.
As her skin cracks in the heat,

she's silent. As we blindly fire flaming arrows,
she watches and we burn down our world.
When nothing is left of us but coal,
she'll sigh and start again.

Air: Sexism

I can't breathe
under the weight of the atmosphere
that pushes me far from my lofty dreams
to crash on earth without wings;

I writhe on the ground
hoping for help from the other birds above,
but they are vultures, circling,
desiring easy pickings;

I am netted by men
who smile as they pluck my feathers
promising equality for all
as they deny me access to the sky;

they pull my blood as ink
feather pens glittering sharp in my lungs, and I cough out
this poem; my final breath crumbling
under an ever-compressing atmosphere.

Current Events

Blood in repaved streets
seeps into our earth's old bones.
Red horizons bloom.

Breathe

Watching the sunset through a crack in the wall,
I cage my hands over my heart,
exhausted from the very effort of each beat.

A red-crowned king is walking
on a path paved with the ruins of cities,
the train of the cloak collecting skeleton trophies.

Here, people have locked themselves inside
for so long that there's a faint reek
of perpetual rot.

I feel a chill race down my bones and look away.
When I turn back,
he's gone.

No sight of footprints.
No sound of footsteps.
Just a shiver and my heart beats.

Beating broadly, loudly, and I am
relieved, right? Yet, I cannot even muster the
energy to stand even though I am
alive. This city is alive
to see the next sunrise if it wants to, if
hope lives. But we shrink away from its sharp
edges.

Bang! Then, A Bullet

punctures my scholarship letter
      crisply pressed
      to show my teacher—
glassy-eyed on the floor.

tears into the wrapping paper
      of a surprise birthday present
      for my neighbor—
blocked from my view by the cabinet.

shreds my graduation party invitations
      meant to be shared
      with my friends—
soundlessly weeping, shaking sobs.

destroys… nothing
that matters
any more.
It only destroys   paper.

Where Our Wings Were

grew a crack once
only the size of a kiss,
but it went to the bone,
and it was hungry.

We fed it with our words
and scraps of broken trust.
We abandoned the leftovers of a relationship
and it grew fat.

We have a crack that didn't start
when we plunged knives into backs
but in the press of our lips on theirs
as crimson dripped down our fingertips.

We fed it with enemy blood,
with a coppery, iron tang
and a hint of sweetness like sugar, like revenge,
that we tasted when we bit our tongues.

We have a crack whose teeth are sharp
whose carnivorous stomach is never filled
which spreads its gaping maw
where our wings were.

Lost

i am stone
and tree
and river
my mother would whisper to me as i slept

she fed me with diamond rivers
that danced over riverbeds
teeming with jeweled fish

she sang to me that the world
is sometimes washed with golden light
and other times bathed in silver snow

she confided in me of oceans coated in stars
that would cling to my skin and make me divine
if only i'd dive in

she regaled me of tales of her other small children,
fragile things with fiery minds that turn
her rocks into glittering glass

who later turn on her till

she screams
(the oceans rise, anguished howls of the wind
bombard the shore)

she sweats
(slickening, sickening
to break feverous drilling)

she shudders
(cities collapse, bones breaking
under the weight of her tears)

i try to breathe
mother
are you....

My Boy

An ocean of ridges, rises, runs,
and rippling plains of sand
that he reached for —
his infinite supply of toys.

My fins kept me flush against him till he pulled ahead;
my teeth tore into screaming mortal flesh;
I touched his sharp smile;
I was his favorite.

He built babylonian towers
simply, surely, in the span of moments
and knocked them down
with a careless finger flick, laughing.

He was mine,
I was his,
forever,
he solemnly swore

with a pinky-promise.
And the years coursed past
in races against the wind
always thinking I'll win till I lose.

Today, finally, I burst ahead
freedom together, equals
for-
never.

Fins and fingers trapped in circles
of blank-eyed white
caught in something
that should be nothing but is:

Humanely built,
humanely left,
humanely scented
of iron and ironic death.

I breathe and choke
gills fighting for air,
I turn to him, my boy, my creator, my everything,
for help,

but he coughs
"I can't race anymore."
He smiles reassuringly
with teeth turned black.

Each breath,
each salty breeze,
offers only smoke
that turns his blood acidic.

He tries and tries and tries
to find a way to survive
but his once-colorful playscapes of coral are bleached
with the chemicals poured down his throat.

He tries to reach for me, rescue me,
but his hands, once swift and strong with sorcery and magic
are tied by the barest chains of plastic;
his fingers still, silent snow-white corpses, as he sobs
I see myself forced to bow to a new master
who builds new towers
of steelly industry
I drift along the shore, belly-up.

"Sorry for breaking my promise"

Old

Does not mean a cane,
rainy bones, or moon-touched hair,
it's change's soft kiss.

Khichdi

Seeds of dal are buried in the rice,
jewels that are dulled by the light,
precious only when tasted.

I look down into the InstantPot;
the steam collects on my face;
my glasses fog up.

I take a deep breath;
I can form the image from the smell,
a little bit spicy, a lot starchy, all home.

My 5 year old self watches Tom and Jerry
on my grandparents' TV
in the corner of the living room.

Eyes glued, mouth open,
a bite is put in my mouth.
I smile and look up at who feeds me.

Dadi's skin glows with the coconut oil she applies daily;
she looks like a fairy godmother out of legend,
her brown skin, a mythical, chocolate jewel.

Now, I close my eyes just for a second,
letting the flavors explode across my tongue
and transport me to the past.

> Dadi's achaar: Infused with the love of her fingers
> packed it into a glass jar to bring on the flight to Atlanta,
> flying on trapezes of flavor.

> Ghee: Clarified butter doesn't sound right,
> it swirls around my mouth like a kathak dancer,
> footsteps that taste of a sweet, soft ladoo.

Dahi: My staple, cool, tangy, and inviting
only when made by Mama's hands
does it give the dancer's music.

Dal: Lentils simmered in the old kadai
form the stage for these flavors to perform
and let the khichdi fill my stomach with delight.

Each performer is ignored when they dance alone;
only the performance they create together
sets off fireworks in my mouth and stomach.

Now, Dadi is a thousand miles away.
Her silent glass canister of achaar
sits on our pantry shelf.

But here, with each spoonful, she's here
a plate in her hand,
smiling as she feeds me.

Frosting

Laughing in the sun
my little brother smiles
and his eyes glitter
like obsidian jewels
softened into the butter he uses
to bake me a birthday cake

he sings off key
and presents me with a lemon cake
frosted with milk and powdered sugar
and it is exactly what I asked for
and the tart cake melts in my mouth
as I stare at his changing face

it shows
someone who isn't so little
as his graphite mark on the wall
inches up closer to mine
someone who isn't so innocent
when he doesn't ask
what the words he hears in movies mean

it shows
a man being made
of the boy who still asks me
did you like it
his face shifts as I watch him
cracking like his voice
which strains to reach the scales he once sung easily

I lick the frosting off of my fingertips
he collects more ammunition
attacking me some more
smearing my face
he sticks out his tongue
our eyes meet
and I smile.

Fall

The trees are dotted with the colors of flowers
in this season not still hot, not yet cold,
so many paths emerge in the wind
for the children leaving to take as they
dare each other to do stunts on the way down.

My mother holds me close and whispers to me
about her own adventures through the wind
and I feel my stalk weakening,
the fibers holding me to her are snapping,
as she pushes me towards flight.

I'm ready for this.
I know so much:
the feeling of splashing in the rain,
the time when the squirrel starts its hoarding of nuts,
the way to sing without words.

I look to my friends, dancing on nearby trees,
they try to shake off their tethers to fly
to the world we have never seen untethered,
counting on each other to stay together
for the millions of things we want to try.

I call my pigments to the surface:
I turn myself yellow,
then red,
then brown,
and I hide away my green heart.

The ground calls,
the world is pushing me,
and my heart pounds as
the wind promises me
a lifetime of flight far away.

Gone

A candle, when it goes out,
leaves nothing behind but a puff
of smoke
that soon dissipates.

The sun, when it crosses the horizon,
gives you no promise that it will return.
You shiver and look at the distant stars,
hoping for warmth soon.

When I left, I told you,
forever, because hope
held by the heart
breaks something when torn out.

My steps in the dirt
have been trampled.
The ring of my laughter has been
carried away by the breeze.

And you wonder, was I ever here?

Roots

After Roadhouse *by Francisco Díaz-Granados*

My roots grip at the water,
shining gold in the light,
hoarding it inside like my ancestors did.
But it fights me like never before
pulls me towards the edge,
threatening to push me over.

My nicks and cuts,
hearts carved into my bones,
stories that engraved themselves onto me,
fall to the water's blinding knives,
and I cannot summon more than the groan
of my branches during autumn.

My bark sloughs off
rivers, valleys, oceans become smooth and flat.
My flowers wilt, their stems drooping,
faces turning brown and dry
as the last of my pollen flies away
to find a sturdier companion.

My grains groan,
they are too old for this,
the decay has long eaten my insides
like it ate my fathers
till the wind turns my body into
a child's toy whistle.

The endless lives inside me
that chittered their dreams to me at night
scamper out on furry paws
jumping towards shore
looking back, but not returning,
waiting by the edge of the land as sentinels.

I fall slowly,
my years shorn off like the imperfections
of a doll made
in a smoke ridden factory
hearing the ringing
of a long forgotten bell.

Squinting

*It's too bright to see
if humanity's sun is
rising or setting.*

Mirrored

"Look at me"

We eat like we are afraid
of plumping into turkeys,
we turn into devoured bones.

"Beautiful"

We cut off our limbs
to sew on new ones,
we become gargoyles.

"Look at you"

We flee to our bathrooms
and wield toiletries like knives;
whittling masks, we cover our-selves.

"Ugly"

We cage ourselves
with the things our eyes see,
we throw away the keys.

"Not good enough"

A sky of mirrors reflects us from every angle;
their cutting voices in the cadence of our own,
serving only to remind us:
we can never become stars.

The Primary Colors of Light

I.   Red

Paint drips
down her arm
to the floor
like blood.

She bends down
with a worn-out towel
to mop it up
as an officer,
two miles away,
washes a stain
into the public drain.

The ruby she painted
glitters wet
in the light of
a tired sun.

She stands up again
looks at it, dissects it for meaning,
but no,
not good enough—
it'll never be good enough.

From the trash,
the wood of the canvas
groans and screams
as it's deformed by the
unforgiving metal.

It is red.

II.   Green

Before the field that came before the forest that came before the
city began to grow,
there was a snail with a big dream, a bug with a big heart, and a
frog with a big toe;
they lived   they died   they decomposed.

Quick! Come! Claim this land, riches galore to be had!
Roots swarmed like soldiers and claimed, with flags and drums,
no man's land:
the rich, brown dirt.

On blood and guts and victory,
their trunks grew strong and mighty.
They fought each other to survive
and helped each other thrive
till they fell to the iron teeth
of a human saw;
they lived   they died   they decomposed.

Quick! Come! Claim this land, riches galore to be had!
Paper from life and paper from death
and humans grew rich
surrounded by the cold shadow
of concrete;
they lived   they died   they decomposed.

Quick! Come! Claim this land, riches galore to be had!
A fresh-faced shoot —
a daisy or grass stalk or clover or mystery —
cracks through concrete
laid generations ago.

Death offers cymbals and claps
at the birth of the cycle anew

because it's seen everything before and
it'll see everything again,
and everything,
it is green.

III.   Blue

When you sigh
and a door inside you opens
for all of your dreams
to escape,

when the sun dips
her hands into paint
and streaks the sky
with color,

when you lie,
crushing the grass
and look up,
searching for a higher being,

when the world
passes by you
like a river
parting around a rock,

when you exhale,
deepening the tired wrinkles
in the corners
of your immortal eyes,

when you close them
and that smile of yours,
glowing with the soft, rippling light
of the world you see,
touches your face,

it is blue.

"Hope is the Thing with Feathers"
- Emily Dickinson

Flying above death
recovering from its wounds
nestling in our hearts

"Binary Compounds Decompose into Separate Elements."

- Chemical Law

Colors, genders, morality, sexuality, our world is no longer binary for each of us are made of a mixture of separate compounds until we die, fall apart into blood and bone, decompose combine, mingle, and our differences turn into dirt, feeding those who follow we are no longer rigidly separate as our walls collapse. Finally, we are at one with our elements.

"We Are All Mad Here"

-Lewis Carrol

full of swirling thoughts, we are caught in the tides of our brain; we do not understand what we are (mortal); we look to other things, shiny distractions, but it comes for us all the time when we have to face the truth, when we understand life is mad just swirling happenings that will leave nothing behind to show — I was here.

"Off With Their Heads"

-Lewis Carroll

Our anger today funnels through machines with no button that says, *off*. It feeds into a burner that grows hotter with our hatred for *everyone else* and their *wrong ideas*. We don't need guillotines to roll heads.

"Why is a Raven like a Writing Desk"

- Lewis Carroll

The sky is pink, and the clouds are made of candy, and it doesn't matter why because I can laugh, my hair can swing in the breeze, and this world simply is wonderful. I can close my eyes and forget. Forget that terrible day, a moment when I saw the ominous shadow of a raven that tore my world to pieces and swept it apart like my life was only paper. Ink everywhere, a broken world, a place that was mine. Lost. I look up at this pink sky I am writing and this paradise is as real as the girl sitting at my desk.

"There is No Greater Agony than Bearing an Untold Story Inside You"

- Maya Angelou

It's a glass sculpture hinting at rainbows, but we forged it clear and white. Set it there (flip it upside down). Make its reaching hands (don't try for more) reach down. It is (only) meant to serve. It has no dreams (just glass, cold and hard) and what greater purpose is there than us? And flip it upside down, because why would it feel agony when we forged its figure with the most prominent brains (extra big!). Happier here than its home (that's a place of death, disease & desire), uncomplainingly (aka happily) bearing the weight of us (we are kings, queens & emperors in new clothes) and an involuntary weight of gratitude (railway tracks, rice & gold). Oh! I forgot, almost left untold the name of this amazing art we created by simply (easily & quietly) removing their story — the "Model Minority". Their story? My story. But, we hid it behind "drive", buried it inside till I don't know what I'm trying to tell you.

31

"And All of This Will be True Unless We Choose to Reverse It"
- Jonathan Reed in *"Lost Generation"*

read quiet and soft.
it's unnecessary to
scream your voice out loud.

War Hides

victory.
I'll do anything to save my
green meadows.
Already filled with blood are your
borders.
Pointless wars define
your country.
My country is defined by
peace.
Morals and spirituality bless
my sovereignty.
An instrument of oppression lies in
your leaders.
I smile only to destroy
the pain of your citizens.
I care not about
what it costs.
Immeasurable is the truth of
my righteousness and goodness.
A lie is
your potential.
This is a war against
evil.
This is my path of
goodness and grace.
This world is not made of
bloody broken promises.

Every Mirror has Another Side

the weight of an ocean of inadequacy
destroys
the strength of my heart
burns through the night till it becomes ashes and
the bonfire full of my regrets and losses
that dances in a fury meant to shatter the ground and
my fragile confidence
that shrivels and succumbs to
the cruel bite of the night
coming out to crush
my hope

Flip the Coin

Possibility is limited.
it is an oft-believed lie that
for the ones in rags who dream
true wealth will come.
the lack of pennies reveals
scant frames and hungry eyes.
riches create worlds with
glistening jeweled palaces.
hope is
cheap.
a pile of gold is
priceless.
character is
useless, like sand
in the wind,
a name
dissolves
justice

Floating on the Waves

Searching, pondering:
what else has been lost to the
unforgiving sea

The Tide

It ebbs and flows
like a heartbeat pumping
faster and faster.

Each droplet, a soldier screaming,
in different tongues, different voices,
your name.

All the voices in the tide reach a crescendo
and move one inch closer
to your feet.

They beg you, on their knees:
Help me find peace after my crimes!
I know You can save my sister!

They try to wound you, eyes full of tears:
Do you not care about people like my son?
Am I not one of your children?

They try to bribe you, hands dripping red gold:
I'll pray every day if you just get me the job...
I'll give you everything if you give me a sign...

Do you not notice the spray
of the tide that washes away
every day?

Do you just close your eyes
to hear nothing but the lullaby
of the waves and sigh?

Or do you listen?

Rust

When ore is mined
from inside the earth's womb
does she cry out for her child?
Or
Does she push him away from her
to see the world, form something new,
and grow a thick skin to injustice?

When we bend it, deform it
hammer it into our image
does it condemn humanity?
Or
Does it grit its teeth
and hope the pain is over soon
so it can look over its new, shined body with pride?

Is it better to be natural?
Is it better to be pure?
Is it better to be innocent?
Or
Is it better to be broken?
Is it better to be destroyed?
Is it better to be hardened to the world?

Than to be left behind
to collect dust
and slowly rust

Once Upon A Time

Stretching out before me
lies a path of echoes
of words stretching on forever
in verses, ink, voices, and rhyme.

It pulls at the fringes of my core
Like my predecessors, storytellers, shapers of the myth

I belong to it

The shapeshifter story emerges
change me, it calls, make me your own
never content to sit and grow old

immortal and ancient,
thousands of voices join
into a crescendo

It is mine
it is theirs
it holds me in its grasp
as it sings the endless tale
of Once Upon A Time...

When We Return
invoking the ghazal

We are stripped beyond bone when we return
Our posturing ridden of when we return

After a lifetime of fighting endless battles
Putting away the sword to rust we return

We sleep through many turns of the clock
Our eyes clear and we awake when we return

We make our futures lie in paper and ink
Yet those futures cease to matter as we return

Moving endlessly as part of life's machine
When we stop, break away, that's when we return

Good or bad, black or white, it all falls away
All of us are nothing when we return

We Contain Multitudes

*Is it lost? Can we
still persevere and contain
hope in multitudes?*

I Wonder

A stream of consciousness

i wonder what makes up the sky   is it clouds of magic or is it
the basic bonds of water   would they taste like cotton candy
sweet and sticky with belief   would they be minty   like
the feel of the wind on a warm summer day   would
they taste like the rain in our dreams   made of
lemondrops and gumdrops   our hands sticky with candy
why is it that only when we sleep we taste happiness   i once
dreamt of a cake made entirely of whipped air   invisible to
the eye   with a spoon stuck up high   but just as I
reached out   to take a bite   lifted the silver spoon to
my mouth   it passed my lips   it fell towards my tongue
and i woke up   to taste   air   and i was disap-
pointed   maybe thats strange   hoping to defy the
laws of science   by the power of my own belief   if
only for a moment   maybe science has doomed us all to lives
with our feet bound to this earth   unable to try and hitchhike
a ride on the sun chariot   or taste the forbidden fruits of
the underworld   or to have faith that a prayer would bring
rain   to the parched desert   instead of melting into a lost
ice cream cone   instead of seeping into the dirt   instead
of being caged on this dry dead sand   if we cry is it a door
to our soul opening or an irritant causing an overflow of salt
water   the ocean is salty   but its also sweet in a different
world   maybe the real world   the ocean would taste
sweet because of all the things it has seen   but when it
looks at our world   imaginary maybe   wrought with
science   the wonder slipping away   the ocean loses its
sweetness   the ocean of milk curdles   and turns to paneer
we arent broken just different   the oceans salt is a seasoning
in our world spicy and hot and sour   we humans werent
meant to be gentle maybe   but what in this world is
maybe the water we drink is poisoned with all the blood   that
we ignore   that finds its way to oceans and seas   un-
til every drop we drink   every drop in our body is

42

polluted   maybe our world is on fire   that every one
of us adds a spark to   screaming out for attention   until
the truths of our existence   what we took for granted   the
fundamentals of existence   burn
maybe the earth that used to nurture us   is dying   and the
cracks that spiderwebbed across mother earth   have become
pits and its only a matter of time before all the bridges between
us   break maybe the air we used to breath
has been stolen   by men with power and money   who let
those of us   who dissent   who scream   who call for change
who claim the right to our own bodies
choke
i wonder   is goodness is doomed to live only in our dreams?

Light

From a bud, a petal pokes out,
and its honeyed scent fills the air;
a leaf is growing, green at last,
ending nature's yellow streak;
jeweled colors...

The birds are clearing out their throats,
for it is time to sing;
chipmunks hidden below the earth's crust
blink as they see the diamond light;
bright-eyed faces...

for the strength and goodness of humans
is blooming

blooming is
humans of goodness and strength

Acknowledgments

First and foremost, I want to thank my family: Mumma, Papa, Shiv, Savi, Dadi, Baba, Nanaji, and Naniji.

Usha Auntie, your first class changed my life and eight years of mentorship later, I cannot thank you enough! Moreover, to Matwaala, Sync, Austin Bat Cave, Mr. Jonathan Waters, Mrs. Tania Pope, Mrs. Rebecca Bingham, Mrs. Cindy Choung, Ms. Tracy Smith, Sophia, Loka, Agni, and all my other teachers and mentors and teammates and supporters till now, thank you!

For Tony, Tate, and the entire Kallisto Gaia team, thank you from the bottom of my heart for everything. We built a book together; that's incredible!

Finally, thank you to everyone reading this book, reading my words, because that is priceless.

"*Once Upon a Time*" was on the Poetry Wall at the Irving Museum and Archives as part of the Beyond Bollywood Showcase. No other poems have been published before in their entirety.